RECESSIONS ARE WHEN MILLIONAIRES AND BILLIONAIRES ARE CREATED.

RECESSIONS ARE WHEN MILLIONAIRES AND BILLIONAIRES ARE CREATED.

By: D.K. Hawkins
Version 1.1 ~December 2022
Published by D.K. Hawkins at KDP
Copyright ©2022 by D.K. Hawkins. All rights reserved.

No part of this publication may be reproduced, distributed, or transmitted in any form or by any means including photocopying, recording, or other electronic or mechanical methods or by any information storage or retrieval system without the prior written permission of the publishers, except in the case of very brief quotations embodied in critical reviews and certain other noncommercial uses permitted by copyright law.

All rights reserved, including the right of reproduction in whole or in part in any form.

All information in this book has been carefully researched and checked for factual accuracy. However, the author and publisher make no warranty, express or implied, that the information contained herein is appropriate for every individual, situation, or purpose and assume no responsibility for errors or omissions.

The reader assumes the risk and full responsibility for all actions. The author will not be held responsible for any loss or damage, whether consequential, incidental, special or otherwise, that may result from the information presented in this book.

All images are free for use or purchased from stock photo sites or royalty-free for commercial use. I have relied on my own observations as well as many different sources for this book, and I have done my best to check facts and give credit where it is due. In the event that any material is used without proper permission, please contact me so that the oversight can be corrected.

The information provided in this book is for informational purposes only and is not intended to be a source of advice or credit analysis with respect to the material presented. The information and/or documents contained in this book do not constitute legal or financial advice and should never be used without first consulting with a financial professional to determine what may be best for your individual needs.

The publisher and the author do not make any guarantee or other promise as to any results that may be obtained from using the content of this book. You should never make any investment decision without first consulting with your own financial advisor and conducting your own research and due diligence. To the maximum extent permitted by law, the publisher and the author disclaim any and all liability in the event any information, commentary, analysis, opinions, advice, and/or recommendations contained in this book prove to be inaccurate, incomplete, or unreliable or result in any investment or other losses.

Content contained or made available through this book is not intended to and does not constitute legal advice or investment advice, and no attorney-client relationship is formed. The publisher and the author are providing this book and its contents on an "as is" basis. Your use of the information in this book is at your own risk.

TABLE OF CONTENTS

TABLE OF CONTENTS 3
INTRODUCTION 5
CHAPTER 1: HOW DO YOU PREPARE FOR A RECESSION? 7
CHAPTER 2: HOW TO BREAK THROUGH THE OBSTACLES 15
CHAPTER 3: SALES GROWTH DURING A RECESSION. 28
CHAPTER 4: MARKETING DURING AN ECONOMIC RECESSION .. 39
CHAPTER 5: ESTABLISH YOUR IDENTITY DURING THE RECESSION. 50
CHAPTER 6: HOW TO GROW YOUR BUSINESS DURING A RECESSION. 54
CHAPTER 7: HOW TO STOP WORRYING AND REDIRECT YOUR ATTENTION TO BUSINESS GROWTH! 58
CHAPTER 8: BE ACTIVE RATHER THAN PROACTIVE 64
CHAPTER 9: STRATEGIES FOR BUSINESS STABILIZATION DURING A RECESSION. 71
CHAPTER 10: HOW GREAT COMPANIES CAN THRIVE EVEN DURING HARD TIMES. 78
CHAPTER 11: GROW YOUR BUSINESS REGARDLESS OF MARKET CONDITIONS. 89
CHAPTER 12: CONCENTRATE ON INNOVATION, NOT RECESSION. 95
CHAPTER 13: STRATEGIES FOR INCREASING SALES DURING A RECESSION. 102

CONCLUSION. 106

INTRODUCTION.

We are all familiar with the negative repercussions of a recession, including unemployment, inflation, and many more but believe me; some good is to be found. In this book, I will describe the advantages of the current economic downturn and how you might start to earn a fortune within the next month.

I'll start this piece with a few facts. During the Great Depression, more millionaires were created than at any other time. Yes, more millionaires were made during one of the worst periods in US history than in all other eras combined. You can ask why this is the case, and the answer is straightforward.

Necessity! It's not an unexplainable phenomenon that supplying what others desire is the easiest way to become a millionaire. Direct sales are merely a byproduct of the economic downturn.

Direct sales are the most reasonable path to financial independence. The Internet is linked with how technology is transforming direct sales. Indeed, the Internet lifestyle is desirable, but there are many prerequisites for success.

You must be committed to what you are doing; else, you will never achieve the life you wish. According to the adage, "you should measure your ego by your financial account," your opinion is worthless if someone has what you desire. Therefore, submit yourself to the larger good.

There are many more benefits of economic recession than initially appear, but you will need a strategy to achieve your goals. If you want to quit your work eventually, fire your boss or simply take a vacation and spend more time with your family, you already possess the desire. Therefore, take the steps discussed in this BOOK. Happy Reading.

CHAPTER 1: HOW DO YOU PREPARE FOR A RECESSION?

What exactly is a Recession?

In economic terms, it is the economy's contraction for at least two consecutive quarters. Businesses are creating fewer Sean John jeans and Cadillac Escalade trucks because American consumers, who account for approximately 70 percent of all economic activity, spend less money than they did six months ago.

As consumers continue to reduce their spending, businesses restrict the production of their goods and services and start to lay off employees to enable them to reduce expenses and maintain profits. Since the economic outlook is bleak, investors are no longer sure that firms will be able to raise profits by selling more products, causing a decline in the stock values of large corporations.

Investors start selling their equities when their confidence wanes to avert future losses. To avoid losses due to subprime mortgages, many investors promptly began selling their equities, resulting in a rapid decline in the stock market's value.

What can you do to safeguard your finances?

Become a Part-Time Entrepreneur.

I advise people to consider ways to increase their income since, once the recession is over and everything is back to normal, you will still have that source of income and may be in a better financial situation.

More significantly, you will discover how to become "recession-proof" by creating many streams of income! It's time to identify your passion or pastime and devise inventive ways to make money doing something you enjoy!

If you don't have substantial capital to invest, borrow money and discover a low-cost product to sell on the weekends to augment your "9-to-5" income. For instance, you can negotiate to purchase the entire inventory of products at a local garage sale at a discount, then resell them at a profit at a local flea market and repeat the process. You would be astounded by the financial outcomes.

As the economy deteriorates, the Federal Reserve will reduce short-term interest rates (e.g., credit cards, auto loans) to encourage individuals to borrow and spend, reviving the economy. As interest rates continue to fall, now is an excellent moment to borrow money to launch a business.

I used credit cards to fund my "weekend hustle" (selling clothes) in college. Before the interest was charged, I would pay off the balance and reinvest the earnings until I had sufficient funds and no longer needed to rely on the credit card. Many credit card companies now offer 0% interest, which is free money to invest; nevertheless, it is advisable to read the fine print and know when the offer expires.

Saving, Saving, Saving!

I know that not everyone has the temperament or risk tolerance to become an entrepreneur. So, what will you do if you aren't a small business owner but a 9-to-5 employee? If you can't be a business, you can at least learn to think like one — decrease expenses!

Examine all your expenses and see where you might save money. Try to negotiate with your service providers, including your barber, hairstylist, dry cleaner, and, if possible, your landlord. After completing college, I exchanged everything.

First, I would determine precisely what that individual liked or desired, then find it cheaper than they were paying and offer to swap my services in exchange. I saved hundreds of dollars per month by bartering for food, rent, dry cleaning, and other services.

Refinance Debt.

Refinancing your debt is another method to take advantage of reduced interest rates this year. When you refinance a loan, the bank or financial institution you choose will pay off your current loan in full and put you into a new loan agreement at a lower interest rate. You might consider refinancing to a lower fixed interest rate if you have a mortgage, auto loan, or credit card debt.

For instance, if you have a $25,000 auto loan with an 8.5 percent interest rate, your new refinancing bank will pay off your old loan by sending a check to your old bank and issuing you a new $25,000 loan with a 6 percent interest rate, which will likely reduce the total cost of the vehicle and your monthly payments.

You should haggle with your credit card company to minimize your interest rate. They will likely cut your interest rate if you have been paying more than the minimum sum and have not been overdue with your monthly payments.

Also, you should contact your credit card issuers every six months in the future to request a lower interest rate as well as a higher credit limit to save money and improve your credit.

Start to Invest.

When is the perfect time to invest in the stock market directly or via a 401(k) or Roth IRA? Yesterday! The goal is to start investing quickly because time is in your favor. According to the news, the stock market is performing poorly, and everyone is losing money. The financial reality, however, is that investing in the stock market creates wealth over the long run.

A few months ago, my uncle phoned me and cried, "The market is declining, and I am losing thousands of dollars. What do you recommend I do?" I just instructed him to purchase other shares. Why? Because you are investing in the American economy for the long term, often between 10 and thirty years, you should be financially secure by that time.

My uncle also forgot that he made thousands of dollars up until this year. The market is currently weeding out all the bad investments from the subprime mortgage crisis and will eventually return to normal, allowing him to make even more money.

If he stopped investing at this time, he would miss out on future returns from an undervalued stock market. Ten to twenty years from now, the stock market's value will be much greater than in 2008.

You must understand that the stock market and the American economy will experience financial ups and downs. Still, as the greatest economy in the world, we will continue to have more financial ups than downs. You must be active in this game of capitalism to profit from the ongoing economic advancement.

Remember that people with a wealthy attitude don't waste time and energy moaning about gas prices; instead, they invest in oil stocks so that as gas prices grow, they continue to benefit.

They are fiscally prepared because they have been pushed to consider many strategies to earn multiple income streams. People with a wealthy mindset don't fear recessions since they are financially literate and can perceive money opportunities where others only see financial devastation.

CHAPTER 2: HOW TO BREAK THROUGH THE OBSTACLES.

How are you faring amid this recession, which has already resulted in the unavoidable unemployment of many unlucky individuals? Every month, do you have enough money to cover all payments yet have much left to spend with your family? Or do you have to tighten your belt to make it till your next paycheck? In other words, do you constantly have more months than money?

Would you prefer a straightforward solution that will soon render this impossible? Then continue reading because I will show you precisely how to achieve that starting today but first, let me explain who is providing you with this free paper and why.

Unless you are already extremely wealthy, the CEO of a Fortune 500 firm, or content to remain poor, you must read this FREE study. It will need a minor financial investment on your part, but the results you will get after you implement the step-by-step action plan we will outline on this page will demonstrate that it was money well spent.

One of the simplest ways to start a home-based business in your leisure time while continuing to work for someone else, till this makes working all week, month after month, year after year for mediocre income redundant, is to determine what people are purchasing the most. What are the hottest things that consumers are clamoring for today?

There will always be a demand for products for which you could receive commission payments from suppliers to help them sell more. Still, the best products to start with are those listed above that only need you to embed a link on your website to their website as an affiliate, which is an agent who acts as a liaison between the seller and the buyer.

There may be millions of affiliates of hundreds of thousands of companies marketing other people's products, but the sad truth is that only a small fraction of them can earn a living wage since they don't know how to succeed.

It is free, or should be free, to sign up as an affiliate and start advertising a product or range of items. Typically, you are also given your website and affiliate ID, whereas everyone else receives the same page, which is often a carbon copy of the company's website. As a result, you are in direct competition with them and will never make money solely from that website.

You are only compensated if someone purchases from you. Most consumers purchase directly from the company's main website because they can spend a fortune attracting many eager purchasers to their site.

You need your unique website that sends your aspiring buyers to the main website where they take the payment, ships the customer the product and e-mail you to make you aware that you have made a sale. They will pay you every two weeks, monthly, or whenever the amount exceeds a certain threshold.

It would be very expensive to send out cheques for payments as small as $3, even though most affiliate payments, especially for successful affiliates, are larger.

If the item sells for $100, you will receive $50 through cheque, direct deposit, or PayPal, which some companies require.

Registering for a PayPal account is free, as is opening a Click Bank account, where you may find numerous in-demand products that can earn you up to 75% of the selling price each sale as an affiliate, albeit you must sell in order to make any money.

When I say "sell," I mean that the messaging on your website generates demand while your company's main website closes the deal. Otherwise, you will be waiting an eternity.

This allows so-called super affiliates to earn astronomical amounts of money while the rest get nothing. They entice eager beavers to their website, capture their e-mail addresses and names, direct them to the company's primary website and create a relationship with them.

Why should people trust you? Virtually no one will purchase from you on their first visit, especially if they do not know who you are. Therefore, it may take numerous e-mails with helpful free advice before they are willing to place their trust in you and buy the goods you suggest.

Furthermore, why should you believe me about that? Since I am not costing you a dime or a penny, if you find what I say to be worthless, all you need to do is delete this message; however, you would be making the gravest mistake possible if you did so without reading further.

Most so-called gurus want you to pay them in advance to learn anything without knowing if what they say is true or if you will make money using the information they provide.

I wish I had a penny for each website or e-mail with the headline "You can make $30,000 in 15 days," as if a beginner could do so. Yes, pigs that can run fast enough can learn to fly.

Someone who has been running their internet business successfully for a year or two and has sold hundreds or thousands of identical products to their devoted consumers can make that money and sometimes much more. Still, if you are a novice, you are merely wishing.

But enough about that; let's move on to how and why you should start doing this. Why should people who are no smarter than you make ten times or more money per day than you while you work yourself to an early death for four to six weeks or more is a question I can easily answer.

It is a reality that some students who had no meaningful grades in school are today multimillionaires, while those who excelled are sweeping the streets for peanuts. Wealth is no longer associated with intelligence, brainpower, or being superhuman. Using the power of the Internet, ordinary individuals often make millions and enjoy a lavish lifestyle with plenty of free time every day.

Many people believe that having more money is bad or wrong, yet they misunderstand why everyone should try to amass substantial wealth. If you are wealthy, you can support many worthy causes and those in most need. However, if you are poor, you can't even help yourself.

I've been poor before and hated it, so I'm now attempting to become wealthy, so I may help others instead of spending all of my money on expensive mansions, vehicles, vacations, jewelry, and watches. Having a large amount of spare cash would make me feel bad if I did not also donate to aid others in dire need.

Consequently, 85 percent of those who win millions on the National Lottery in the United

Kingdom typically spend all penny within a few years and finish up poorer than before. They waste all their money on pleasures they can't afford without investing in anything that will ensure a steady flow of income.

When they receive their riches, they are given plenty of helpful advice but are greedy and refuse to listen. On the other hand, people who become affluent through their businesses almost always remain wealthy because, upon learning how to create money, they become motivated to earn more to maintain their fortune.

Even if their business fails during difficult times, they often relaunch and become wealthy again because they know what to do and learn from their experiences.

So let's start being a businessperson and break free from the chains of wage-slave dependence that have prevented you from achieving your birthright, a fair standard of living.

What is the step-by-step strategy that we are employing? I will tell you immediately.

STEP 1.

Determine what you are most interested in doing or working on, as doing something you enjoy is more likely to motivate you to work than a job you do for the money alone.

Check whether many individuals are searching for information or a solution to an issue similar to your passion or expertise.

Can you locate and provide them with what they need?
How many other websites already perform this function, and can you perform it better?

Are searchers willing to pay for answers; if other websites compete, there must be an opportunity to generate revenue.

Assuming there are too many websites, it may be preferable to find another hungry, eager market to serve or to become an affiliate of the top-selling site if they have an affiliate sign-up page.

Once you've identified a small amount of competition, determine how many individuals seek that information online each month.

You must locate a niche in that market where few people provide information or aren't providing it adequately.

Suppose you enjoy playing golf. If you enter "golf" into Google, you will receive over a million unusable results because hundreds of websites sell golf equipment, promote golf courses, and offer golf lessons. Therefore, you must find a market segment with significantly less competition in order to increase your chances of making money.

If you attempt to "fix your golf slice," your numbers will start to improve, but you must devote a lot of time to this essential research; otherwise, you won't be able to quit your work soon.

A niche is a highly specialized market segment; if you specialize, you have a far better chance of launching your first firm. Once you have identified a likely group of people seeking answers but are having difficulty locating them, you can provide them with what they need by conducting other Internet research.

There are many categories on Click Bank where you can discover what others are purchasing. Amazon and eBay are also excellent sources. Don't forget to determine the number of Google searches utilizing key terms. The list of golf-related phrases includes " golf books, golf, how to play golf, how to play like a pro," etc.

After deciding what to base your first business on, find someone having an affiliate link on their website, sign up, and develop your website with a summary of the product's benefits, which you should purchase and use yourself. Then you can compose a book describing how your life has vastly improved since purchasing the product.

Make this as enticing as possible so that everyone who reads it will want it, but only if what you say is true. If you try to fake it, they will catch on, and you won't make any money, so focus on the benefits rather than the features and purchase only what you truly need.

A vehicle's six-speed automatic transmission is irrelevant. It is beneficial to inform them that the gearshifts are so smooth that you hardly notice them. Nobody gets excited about leather seats, but it's a plus if you say you drove 350 miles and arrived smelling like a daisy.

The benefits, not the features, motivate consumers to accept your offerings. It's a case of "what's in it for me," since no one will care if you need the money unless they believe their lives will be better.

Therefore, what do people want today that you can provide and for which they are prepared to spend money? Consider what would make your life significantly better. Is there a way to earn much more money without working for a long time?

Many individuals hunt for answers there, but the majority are finally duped too many times or are discouraged when they realize that, at least initially, hard work would be required.

Those who seek simple solutions, large sums of money, and little or no effort will constantly fall for "get rich quick" schemes and become poorer. The reality is that there is no easy shortcut to wealth, and only those who expect everything to be handed to them still fall for such schemes. Therefore, how hard are you willing to work during your six hours of spare time at home each week?

Some effort now will turn your life from ordinary to extraordinary; isn't that worthwhile? Are you prepared to go for it, or are you content to continue doing what has failed to provide you with the life you desire? You have a choice, so choose the right one, or you'll always wonder, what if?

CHAPTER 3: SALES GROWTH DURING A RECESSION.

There is always a positive aspect to every circumstance. While I acknowledge that a recession might affect your firm, it does not dictate its result. You control this, but few business owners comprehend how to do so. Once this insight is ingrained in your being and operation, increasing sales during a recession become more probable; it becomes a pattern that transcends boom and bust!

In my opinion, a recession emphasizes and amplifies the inefficiencies and poor practices of a business that was permitted to survive in a market that was heading upward.

In good times, most firms are content with a satisfactory return on investment, and few recognize that they could be earning significantly higher sales if they realize that the internal dynamics of their business aren't precise.

Also, good times tend to promote "laziness" in business when there is little motivation to learn, push the limits of sales growth or critically evaluate systems/actions that do little to increase sales.

Recessionary times also tend to expose the absence of ideas and solutions of many of our so-called business "leaders." Leaders and innovators are the ones who pioneer and continuously push the boundaries of their respective industries. Sadly, there are so few genuine leaders and innovators.

They act this way in good and bad times because they are who they are. They are always seeking ways to increase sales. They recognize that the current state of their business is a direct result of actions and decisions taken in the past. If the outcome is unsatisfactory, they change their decisions and activities to generate favorable results.

Leaders and innovators make up a very small portion of the business world. Consequently, they can continue to generate sales growth. Still, they aren't difficult to discover in any market - their enterprises are the odd few that always appear active, always have clients, and are typically recognized as the market leader in their industry. As stated, though, these are a select handful.

Why is this so?

What do they know or do that is distinctive?

The straightforward explanation is that the owners of such prosperous enterprises don't think or act like most other owners. These folks are involved in all facets of their firm. They have extremely high expectations of themselves, their employees, and their business.

These profitable firms aren't the result of chance. They make distinguishing distinctions that the majority don't. It is as simple as looking at the same item from a new perspective.

The most effective technique to make you comprehend is to ask you the following questions:

1. Do you have in-depth knowledge of your products/services?
2. Are you aware of your business's unique selling points?
3. Are you aware that 1% of your actions can provide 98% of your revenue?
4. Are you aware that losing clients can result in increased profits?
5. Are you certain that your business is the greatest in the local market?
6. Do you have in-depth knowledge of your local market?
7. Do you actively seek change?
8. Are you aware of the vast distinction between business owners and entrepreneurs?
9. Do you know your current financial standing?
10. Do you realize there's no such thing as competition?
11. Are you aware that all answers to all questions can be found within your organization?

Positive and prompt responses to these questions identify leading-edge businesses. They choose companies with a mission, and a solid basis focused on expansion.

If you responded "no" to any of these questions, I would imply that your business isn't "anchored down" to a stable foundation and is likely being carried by the winds of the recession. The good news is that your company has the greatest potential for rapid and robust sales growth - EVEN IN THIS ECONOMICAL CLIMATE!

Let's examine the first question in greater detail.

The first step for individuals working in the cafe industry is to examine the links in the supply chain of every product and collect the most up-to-date and accurate information regarding which products/suppliers offer absolute consistency and the best quality.

As soon as a sales decline occurs, the owners immediately respond to cut all operating expenses. While attempting to cut operating expenses is commendable, doing so at the expense of product consistency and quality will directly and negatively impact sales.

In addition, some products need greater processing expertise to ensure total uniformity and the best quality. Once a product, such as coffee, has been compromised based on price, its consistency and quality are typically diminished further throughout processing.

Why is this so?

More often than not, there is a direct correlation between organizations prioritizing cost-cutting and a lack of employee training. When a barista lacks the expertise and abilities necessary to prepare coffee beans with absolute consistency and the greatest possible quality, the final customer receives a substandard product with no local market differentiation.

I have witnessed many firms inadvertently generating a point of differentiation with their inconsistent and subpar coffee.

As previously said, the front line is but one link in the coffee supply chain. If any link lacks total consistency at the highest possible quality, a company's capacity to increase sales quickly and fast falls substantially.

Superior expertise, continual comparative analysis, and an unrivaled dedication to quality may initially "cost" a corporation, but the return on sales growth is nothing short of remarkable. Would a growth rate of 100 to 1,000% per year pique your interest?

For this type of performance improvement, I would prefer to refer to this initial 'cost' as a 'leveraged investment.' Having worked with over one thousand coffee-based enterprises. This simple strategy has repeatedly proven effective.

I've discovered that the greatest barrier to a shift in emphasis is the difficulty of business owners to accept that investing a little more to get the highest quality products on the market (rather than cutting back) may significantly increase sales. Simply put, they don't believe the growth rates I have cited are possible.

Old habits die hard. If I were accustomed to average returns over some years and observed that other firms around me accomplished the same, I would consider average returns the norm.

The reality is that a business can NEVER save its way to success; rather, it must SELL its way to success, and the greatest way to do so is by offering customers a better product at a reasonable price. Notice that I did not need that your things be inexpensive?

Being the cheapest product in town draws cheap customers, increasing your staff's workload for little return. Adding value for money attracts those prepared to pay for it and increases your return.

Despite this, it isn't sufficient to assume that the most expensive products on the market have the highest quality. A mix of elements makes one product superior to another for your company. Factors including:

• The level of market maturity, i.e., how sophisticated consumers' tastes are for the product in issue.
• Comparative analysis is undertaken objectively and through a focus group; it is never conducted subjectively.
• The manufacturer's skill level, expertise, and experience.
• The quality of the first raw materials, often known as the origins or antecedents.
• Perhaps most importantly, which product fulfills the enterprise's overarching strategic aim? (I assume it is revenue growth in most cases, but this has not always been the case.)

As you can see, much more labor and thought are necessary than most business owners imagine or dare to pursue. Regardless of the recession, rapid and accelerated sales growth is the reward for following through and exploring the details behind each question to the same degree as the first.

It is feasible to make your business resistant to ANY external variables through concentration and diligence. This includes economic conditions and consumer purchasing trends. The questions above provide the information necessary to develop your firm in that direction.

Top-tier operators know that their firms' internal state determines their sales results and the overall profitability of their businesses. To start moving your business to this "ultimate" state, it is essential to acquire cutting-edge information and implement it within your organization. Only the knowledge, systems, and activities that increase sales quickly should be sanctioned. Everything else is time and effort wasted.

Furthermore, it is essential never to convince yourself that your knowledge is sufficient. No one ever does, and understanding this ensures that you and your organization will continue to seek out new opportunities and progress positively despite constantly shifting market conditions.

Ironically, it is simple to comprehend yet challenging to implement. The more you and your employees learn, organize, and utilize that knowledge, the higher your sales will be. This is why there are so few enterprises at the top.

All others suffer disproportionately during recessions. I hope I have prompted you to consider how your firm now runs. In this economic situation, nothing other than a rise in sales will prove that you are implementing some of the above suggestions.

CHAPTER 4: MARKETING DURING AN ECONOMIC RECESSION.

Whether or not a recession will occur is still up for dispute. However, it does raise a sensitive issue for many firms. Should you maintain marketing expenses or defer them till the economy improves?

Let Your Brand Sell Itself.

When the economy's stability is in question, the initial response of many businesses is to reduce their marketing activities until the bull market returns. There is no better time to market than during a genuine or perceived recession.

During the 1990-1991 economic recession, John Vanderzee, former advertising manager for the Ford division of Ford Motor Company, stated, "Anyone who retrenches due to the recession has his head buried in the sand." Vanderzee then noted that investing in marketing amid a recession is essential.

A recession might be viewed as an opportunity rather than a death sentence. Customers are assessing their alternatives carefully and will continue seeking affordable, high-quality products and services as they become more cost-conscious. You are already ahead of the curve if your product or service is synonymous with value.

In addition, your competitors may be less noticeable, as many businesses fail to recognize the opportunity and reduce their marketing expenditures. As a result, they forfeit market share opportunities. As a result, your ongoing marketing activities stand out and are more likely to be heard because there is less market buzz.

During a recession, a strong brand may pay huge benefits, greatly boosting the success of your marketing activities. Suppose your brand displays value to your audience, is well-managed, establishes an emotional connection with your target audience, and instills loyalty. In that case, you will likely fare well during any supposed recession.

The Retirement Red Zone campaign by Prudential is one example. It addresses the retirement concerns of consumers and reassures the audience that they may reach their retirement goals despite the current economic climate.

Utilizing television, radio, and print advertisements, the campaign directs consumers to the Prudential website. They can interact with personal advisors and access different instructional tools, resources, and information on their websites.

Don't fear if your brand doesn't fulfill the standards mentioned above. Now is an excellent time to increase visibility (often amid less competition). Take the time to perfect your brand and communicate with your audience to emphasize its worth.

Also, you can have a well-known brand yet a superior product or service. You can question whether or not your audience will continue to "indulge" when times are difficult. If you have effectively defined and strengthened your brand, your core customers will continue to purchase. Consider Tiffany's as an example.

Despite economic recessions, Tiffany's continues to prosper. People continue to purchase despite the price since the brand's quality, and enduring appeal has been bolstered. The packaging's robin's-egg blue hue is instantly identifiable, even without the brand's name. It communicates the brand without using words.

You think of hope when you see an envelope or package from Tiffany's. Promise. Something of worth and sophistication Tiffany's items may be expensive, but they represent quality and evoke powerful, pleasant feelings in their target market.

In addition, there are options to revitalize your brand. Utilize this opportunity to reeducate your employees on the importance of brand loyalty and how it helps to sustain sales during economic downturns.

This is just what Tylenol achieved and transferred its internal devotion into outward marketing. The corporation created a campaign that featured its employees promoting the brand and expressing their loyalty to the organization.

Also, you might refocus your brand to appeal to a larger or new audience. Dove's Campaign for Real Beauty addressed society's impossible and unreasonable beauty standards for women by declaring, "You are beautiful as you are."

In support of this campaign, Dove encouraged all women to recognize their natural beauty. The campaign engaged the public by allowing them, among other things, to tell their story, build their campaigns for true beauty, and participate in contests and blogs. As a result, the audience assisted in promoting the Dove brand.

Remember that the economy will eventually recover. Consistent marketing during a recession helps maintain momentum. It leaves an indelible stamp on the memory of your target audience, making them more inclined to return to a more stable economic climate. Those who abandon or limit their marketing efforts during a recession have a considerably more difficult time rebounding once the economy recovers.

Create lemonade from lemons.

Your existing marketing strategy must account for economic recessions, and there is no one-size-fits-all solution. You must examine your company's market brand equity and the worth of your products/services to find the optimal method. Nevertheless, here are some strategies to consider:

Reiterate the worries of the audience.

Then, demonstrate how your product or service may alleviate their concerns. Before purchasing, your audience would seek guarantees that your product or service will give great benefits and good value. Quaker Oats redesigned its product in response to the economic downturn of the early 1990s, which plagued it with dismal sales.

First, they engaged the trustworthy, grandfatherly actor Wilford Brimley as a spokesperson. Then, they emphasized that oats were a cheap source of protein, with a bowl costing only nine cents. The outcome was a rise in sales.

Concentrate on a niche market.

Determine which sector of your target market needs your services the most. These customers are more likely to be receptive to your message. Find ways to provide added value, such as through extra or extended services. This will help you earn their business and inspire trust and loyalty due to your adaptability in a challenging business environment.

Tap an untapped market.

We work on an increasingly global scale every day. Seek for previously untouched markets, especially those in foreign countries. As nations such as China continue to establish a presence in the global economy, two things will occur: spending will increase, and these nations will purchase more western goods and services. Utilize this opportunity to get a competitive advantage.

Demonstrate your indispensable nature to customers.

Even if you build it, that doesn't guarantee that people will come. Firms must demonstrate their worth to customers, especially during a recession.

Provide solid case studies, examples of how your target's clients would benefit from your services/products, and client success statistics to support your value proposition. A reputable brand exudes value, thereby fostering client loyalty.

Appeal to the prospects' emotions.

It isn't a coincidence that successful campaigns appeal to customers' brand loyalty and emotions. Wendy's admitted that the recession of the 1990s was harsh but that you could still eat well at their restaurant. Hamburgers were cooked to order using freshly ground beef. The abundant and nutritious salad bar was an all-you-can-eat option.

Throughout that period of economic hardship, their sales remained consistent. Despite being highly effective, you must ensure that your message is authentic, reflects the values and behaviors of your target audience, and is simple to relay.

Why? Because a message that is highly visual and emotionally charged is more likely to have a ripple effect as customers disseminate brand awareness. In essence, your clients and prospects become a marketing vehicle.

Bridge the communication gap. In business, technology has eclipsed the importance of human interaction. No matter how advanced technology becomes, it can't replace the strength of human ties. Utilize this strategy to meet with your customers and qualified leads in person.

Ask them about their present worries and obstacles and how you might assist them. Listening attentively and assisting clients in resolving their problems go a long way toward retaining market momentum.

Consider your goods or service in a new light. Your products or services may have been successful in the past. You can't rely on a "same old, same old" mindset during economic downturns. Reexamine your product or service to identify novel applications or benefits for the customer.

During the recession of 1990-1991, Kraft Foods promoted their A-1 Steak Sauce as an excellent condiment for hamburgers in addition to sirloin steak. During that period, consumers were less likely to consume filet mignon and more likely to ingest ground beef. Therefore, this was a wise decision.

Spend money on items and services that thrive in a recession. During the same economic downturn, Dow Chemical Company shifted its marketing budget from Glass Plus cleaner to Ziploc freezer bags, a then-new product line. The company highlighted the ability of these bags to keep the freshness of leftovers. Again, a clever move, as an increasing number of consumers spent less and wasted less.

Evaluation and implementation of effective branding and marketing strategies can help you maintain revenue during difficult times. In truth, despite the gloomy forecasts, you can expand your brand if you construct and advertise it appropriately.

Recessionary Times Demand Proactive Actions.

In difficult times, building trust with your customers, comprehending their values and habits, and remaining visible with a message that meets their problems is essential. If you continue to establish and manage the market value of your brand, your company will be able to withstand any economic slump.

The possibility of a recession can prompt many individuals to act reactively. Instead, adopt a proactive stance and discover opportunities for your business to capitalize on this situation. Doing so will make your business stronger and, perhaps, with a few new consumers.

CHAPTER 5: ESTABLISH YOUR IDENTITY DURING THE RECESSION.

The worldwide economic recession has resulted in the demise of many of the world's largest corporations and organizations, from airlines to financial institutions. Because he worked for one of these businesses or groups, this is most likely the reason why your neighbor is usually at home now.

The rise of the astute businessperson.

Reality dictates that there is no such thing as job security. Repossessions of homes are on the rise, and layoffs are growing commonplace. People are losing faith in themselves more so than in their bosses. Any little business is also vulnerable if significant market leaders are susceptible to the economic slump. Is this correct?

While this is true to some degree, a certain intelligent entrepreneur will emerge during this gap period, a time of financial uncertainty for individuals, families, enterprises, and organizations. During this period, many intelligent individuals will start to prosper.

It has always been argued that a recession is a perfect time to start a business. During this moment, businesses that sell luxury products and services start to function poorly, while those that sell necessities start to perform well. I believe now is the perfect time to create one, even though this may appear foolish and risky to most people.

You can capitalize on the fact that your neighbor is unemployed by recognizing that thousands of other individuals are in the same circumstance. Without intending it negatively, you can establish your own business by delivering a product or service that the market needs.

Most people feel they can't start a business at this time because all the major companies are failing, so they presume and infer they will fail as well. Again, there is no such thing as "I can't" or "We can't" because we are all human and competent. Who would have guessed that any of these huge players would collapse like Goliath? No one is present.

Now is the opportunity to establish oneself as a brand.

If you want to launch your own business and establish yourself as a brand, now is the time to do so. While most firms are losing money, it doesn't always follow that you will as well.

Start a firm that provides a product or service that people already need and can't live without. Remember that consumers have reduced their spending and changed their spending habits.

We spend more of our money on goods we need that are valuable to us. If you start a business selling a product or service that people don't want or value, you can lose money and fail.

Instead of lamenting and worrying about the recession and telling yourself, there are no jobs, take advantage of the crisis by launching your own small business and branding yourself as a successful entrepreneur who rose to prominence amid the worst economic depression since World War II.

CHAPTER 6: HOW TO GROW YOUR BUSINESS DURING A RECESSION.

Despite the gloom and doom, astute business owners are preparing for the eventual economic comeback. As clients cut back, sales cycles lengthen, and revenues decline, the temptation to drastically reduce marketing, sales, and customer service efforts are enormous.

In any case, the phone may be ringing less, customers may be spending less, and it is difficult to absorb the ongoing expenditures of marketing, sales, and customer support. Now is the time to remain steadfast and expand.

Studies have repeatedly demonstrated that companies who continue or expand their marketing and customer service during a recession win market share and emerge stronger when the crisis ends.

That doesn't mean you should just spend recklessly. However, there are three critical areas in which you should spend now to propel your organization to the next level throughout the recovery.

During difficult economic times, the marketing budget is the first to be slashed by enterprises. However, in actuality, such a maneuver just increases the pain. In a few months, your future success will be determined by the marketing and advertising resources you allocate today. Demand doesn't necessarily disappear during a recession, but sales cycles prolong as gratification is delayed.

As your competitors reduce their budgets, maintaining yours will increase your share of voice in your chosen media and your customers' minds. To push the limit, seize this opportunity to acquire premium ad slots formerly held by competitors or to test out marketing strategies you've had in the back of your mind. You likely have more time to dedicate to them at this point.

1. Customer Service - Another effective method for capitalizing on a recession is to improve customer service. You can conduct less business, but that only increases the value of each potential and existing client. Allowing your consumers to navigate a labyrinth of touch-tone options or greeting them with a voicemail box may save you money in the short term but could cost you in the long run.

2. Consider hiring a company that offers live telephone answering or, even better, local, off-site receptionist services where your calls are answered live and customers are serviced. Calls can be discretely announced and connected to you in real time. Some receptionist firms will also organize appointments for you on the spot.

3. Systems - You should prioritize your sales and customer service systems during a recession. Now is the time to build a system for supporting consumers in person and over the phone.

If you have been utilizing a sales and customer service system, you can wish to assess and improve it.

Instilling consumer confidence by providing them with a consistent, polished, professional experience when contacting your firm.

Customers are more willing to spend their hard-earned money with your company if they have greater confidence (especially during difficult economic times). Having a confident demeanor when few people do so provides credibility for your business.

When the economy improves, and pent-up demand for goods and services is released, investments in the proper areas of your organization may yield favorable returns.

CHAPTER 7: HOW TO STOP WORRYING AND REDIRECT YOUR ATTENTION TO BUSINESS GROWTH!

In business, as in life, you must know that you obtain what you concentrate on. If you focus on what you want, you will receive it; similarly, if you focus on what you do not wish to, you will also receive it. A client of mine recently stated plainly, "People are talking themselves into a recession."

You will likely experience anxiety, stress, dread, etc. if you concentrate on something you do not desire. Remember that worry is your mind's way of reminding you to focus on what you want.

A self-actualizing prophecy.

Too many individuals are so preoccupied with what they don't want and wish to avoid that they fail to recognize what they can have and the opportunities that exist in the present.

How frequently do you consider the worst-case scenario or what could go wrong, and when it occurs, you remark, "I knew it would happen"? It became a self-fulfilling prophecy because it has been scientifically demonstrated that the mind cannot distinguish between vivid imagery and reality. On a bigger scale, the same holds for the economy.

I have witnessed economic forecasts become self-fulfilling prophecies. When a sufficient number of consumers and businesses accept economic forecasts and alter their behavior accordingly, the forecasts are realized.

Consumers and corporations change their purchasing and investment decisions based on their level of future optimism. When pessimistic economic expectations are prevalent, consumer and company behavior is modified accordingly, and spending and investment decline. In contrast, when boom predictions abound, confidence, spending, and investment soar, and we as a society generate boom times.

I've recently had numerous unique encounters in retail outlets. Even at networking gatherings, I have witnessed some business owners engage in a cynical discourse when questioned about their company. I watched how the staff's pessimistic outlook affected their behavior and the quality of their client service.

Due to their preoccupation with doom and gloom, they utterly miss possibilities to form relationships with other firms and create referral and cross-promotional opportunities. They are generating a self-fulfilling prophecy; who wants to conduct business with or refer to negative people?

Like attracts like. To attract good individuals and opportunities, you must first exude positivity. So pay special attention to your and your team's attitude during this moment. If you are a team leader, maintain a focused attitude (and encourage your team members to do the same) so that their service levels to existing and new clients remain high.

This is now more vital than ever for setting oneself apart from the competition. With a positive outlook, you will be better able to see and seize opportunities when they arise. Which self-fulfilling prophecy would you wish your business to create?

Regaining Control.

Focusing on what you can influence is the best method to regain control of your business and the events occurring around you. You can control your thoughts, feelings, and actions (including how you respond to situations and people).

Focusing on others, events, or circumstances beyond your control may lead to frustration. When you concentrate on what is under your control, you feel happier and more capable of capitalizing on chances.

Here is a robust approach to help you focus on your goals and take action:

1. Consider an upcoming event about which you are uncertain or anxious, such as a presentation, a promotion, a meeting, etc.
2. Clarify your desired outcome for the event.
3. Imagine a movie screen before you and envision yourself as an actor or actress in the movie depicting the future occurrence.
4. As you watch the film, imagine the situation unfolding exactly as you would like, hearing the discussions you would like to hear, and experiencing the emotions you would like to experience.
5. Observe how you now feel better about the occasion and anticipate it.

Highly successful entrepreneurs and athletes visualize a good meeting or game using this strategy. According to research, athletes who visualize rehearsing and having a successful game perform as well on game day as athletes who physically rehearsed and practiced before the game.

Imagine how you would feel if you took charge of your life and focused on what you can control, as well as the impact this would have on the growth and success of your business!

CHAPTER 8: BE ACTIVE RATHER THAN PROACTIVE.

Most firms are examining their spending during the current economic crisis but are unwilling to reevaluate their overall financial condition. Instead of modifying their business operations or reach, they will cut costs, lay off employees - generally starting with sales - and bury their heads in the sand until they see signs of recovery.

That is one approach, but it may not be the most effective. For those who are receptive to alternative perspectives, here is another way to see the current situation:

Focus initially on customer service.

Call your consumers and discuss their specific circumstances. Ask how the economic downturn will affect their business, comparable to discussing the 600-pound elephant in your living room. Ask them how you can assist them in expanding their business despite the recession. Ask them about their dream client and how you could facilitate an introduction.

When the economy is undergoing difficulty, your consumers are your greatest asset. Ensure that you care for them or that they may seek employment elsewhere when the economy changes.

Predict their needs.

During a period of slow business, you might provide complimentary Word, Outlook, and Excel training to your customers' staff. Taking an hour to plan a webinar for your clients can go a long way toward demonstrating your commitment and sensitivity to their needs.

Avoid making decisions based on fear.

It is acceptable to downsize, but you should not do so out of fear. Any decision made reactively and out of fear will often not produce the optimal outcome.

Historically, more millionaires were created in the 1930s following the Stock Market crisis. Why?

The possibility is for sale.

Right now is an ideal opportunity to vary your product. If you have not previously supplied backup services to your end users, this may be a wonderful chance for you to start developing a marketing strategy to do so.

Most of the individuals you collaborate with know that the economy will recover. In addition, they are likely highly interested in addressing their inefficiencies, making this the ideal time to speak with them about improving their IT efficiency.

What are your primary concerns?

Don't make excuses. Both lack of time and lack of funds are merely excuses.

Your best friend's wedding is approaching. The wedding will take place on a private beach in Hawaii. Your wealthy friend will supply you with a round-trip flight ticket and beach accommodations. Also, all food and beverages are complimentary; the only need is to board the aircraft. There is only one flight that departs for Hawaii at 5:30 a.m.

If you miss the flight, you can't attend the wedding. Oh, and you'll collect $10,000 for boarding the aircraft. There is no possibility that you will miss that flight unless you have decided not to attend the wedding.

What is your primary motivation for engaging in business? Are you regularly engaging in the most profitable business expansion activities?

Most individuals will find the time to pursue their interests. If building your business is no longer your passion and value, you should leave the industry. Your company is only as robust as its weakest link.

What is your most valuable asset?

You should evaluate why your number one asset isn't your clients.

The contacts you've cultivated are your income source and market intelligence. Most business entrepreneurs perform well at the start of their ventures but lose touch once they experience success. This is a general trend that I observe across all industries but can be exacerbated in the IT industry due to the fulfillment aspect of service delivery.

Are you maintaining communication with your customers?

When the economy starts to stagnate, businesses find it far more difficult to network their way into new prospects and start to believe that creating new firms is impossible.

Despite this, most firms discover that a consistent approach makes it easier to acquire new clients. Choose an activity for which you will schedule time each day or week. Make a specified number of daily calls to current clients, for instance, or schedule a coffee or lunch meeting with colleagues.

Improve your marketing and sales skills.

Throughout the history of our economy, things often deteriorate before they improve. However, they typically improve. It is essential to work hard today so that when things improve, you can reap the benefits of your efforts. The perfect use of your energy and time is to improve your marketing and sales skills.

Most IT business owners would agree they aren't good in sales, and those who claim to be good aren't that good. Most of us in sales face a constant uphill battle to improve and avoid making typical errors.

Let's say you learn one new approach per month that helps you close one new deal. That is twelve recent sales each year that you would not have received if you had not invested in sales training. Even if you just close six new agreements per year, it is extremely clear that this investment will generate an immediate return.

In the long run, the organizations that do well in marketing now will be more successful.

According to most marketing specialists, 17 to 29 touches are required before a consumer is ready to purchase. The optimal moment to initiate a marking plan was six months ago; the second-best time is now.

Utilizing low-cost, high-volume, targeted touches is the most effective method for building a new customer base. As more individuals research online, your website will become the most effective tool for acquiring new customers.

Focus your education on creating auto-responders, evaluating Web analytics, and automated marketing tactics that make it simple for prospects to engage with your products and services.

CHAPTER 9: STRATEGIES FOR BUSINESS STABILIZATION DURING A RECESSION.

My friend Roseline called me yesterday to seek my opinion on what her accountant had just told her. Roseline was instructed to develop a "survival plan" for her firm. She resisted doing so and sought my caution and opinion.

Roseline was unhappy. In addition to reducing expenses, her accountant advised her to consider laying off one or two employees, eliminating sick and personal days, and reducing everyone's wages.

She is aware that many small business owners are currently receiving this advice. However, she was intrigued as to whether this was the best suggestion. Is there alternative guidance to consider?

Recessions are typically difficult. Currently, adversity prevails. However, being in a recession doesn't give you permission to take dramatic action or make stupid business judgments. No. Now is the moment to carefully assess the steps necessary to stabilize your firm without impeding its growth.

Before making any "survival plan" decisions, you owe it to your company to evaluate these ten strategies.

Ten Strategies for Stabilizing Your Business During a Recession.

1. Don't reduce your prices.

When the economy slows, reducing your prices is the worst thing to do as a small startup. Many small business owners worry and lower pricing. Once you cut your rates, it becomes more challenging to raise them in the future. Economies fluctuate. Keep your prices unchanged.

2. Avoid giving deep discounts.

If you normally offer a 10% discount to repeat clients and suddenly offer a 20% discount, your consumers will assume they can now bargain rates because they know you can and will go lower. You can't go back in time. You don't wish for this to occur. Maintain your path. Maintain the existing discount.

3. Think small and sell big.

Instead of cutting pricing, inventive small company entrepreneurs are repackaging their products and services to present clients with lower prices. This is a wise decision. Instead of reducing the cost of your products and services, make them more accessible by putting them in smaller, more appealing containers.

4. Offer other payment alternatives.

Consider offering alternative payment choices. Some small business owners will benefit from promoting their products or services with an extended payment plan, while this strategy isn't for everyone. Again, avoid reducing your price.

5. Improve your reputation.

There is no better moment than now to cultivate your reputation. Now is the moment to become a known authority in your profession by publishing a book, hosting a weekly radio program, or speaking at industry events if you aren't already.

Becoming an expert will increase your income, permit you to charge more for your services, and encourage more people to buy from you.

6. Take charge of your thoughts.

The first stage is recognizing what you do and doesn't have control over. While you can not influence the U.S. economy, you have control over the level of risk and exposure your organization has to the economy. Especially during difficult moments, you must exert mental control.

Choose the business strategy you will adopt based on what you can influence.

7. Employ a reasonable frame of mind.

This is a period of uncertainty and worry for many individuals. This doesn't mean, however, that you should start making emotional and irrational decisions. If you've had a small business for any length of time, you're aware that an emotional and irrational approach did not get you to where you are today and won't get you to tomorrow's destination.

8. Adopt a reasonable perspective.

Before making each major business choice, ask yourself, "Am I making a rational or emotional conclusion?" Ignore what other people are doing. Consider the long-term viability of your company while determining which costs to eliminate.

9. Develop an eye for opportunity.

The key to surviving this recession and previous economic hardships is developing an eye for opportunities. Instead of retreating, start searching for chances. There are still many available. In the end, the millionaires of 2012 will be those who recognized possibilities today and seize them.

10. Adopt an alternative style of thinking.

The media would have you believe that the economic downturn threatens everyone and everything. This just isn't the case. To evolve beyond the current circumstance, you must see beyond it.

Consider the 94% of the population who are employed rather than the 6% who are unemployed. Just because there is a recession in the United States doesn't mean you must also experience a mental recession. Change your thinking. Modify your production.

Concentrate on what you wish to expand.

You have the same twenty-four hours as everyone else. What can you do to expand your business during those hours? What you concentrate on grows. What can you focus on that will multiply, expand or expand? What can you do now to grow your business in the future?

To dismiss or not to dismiss? That isn't the issue. It isn't the answer to reduce staff hours, eliminate sick days or reduce the budget simply because other small business owners are doing so.

We are experiencing a recession. We will emerge from the recession. Before making any "survival plans," consider these ten strategies for stabilizing your firm, which won't impede your future success but improve it.

CHAPTER 10: HOW GREAT COMPANIES CAN THRIVE EVEN DURING HARD TIMES.

"Recession" is one of the most misinterpreted and harmful English words! Its easy use elicits powerful emotional responses from customers and businesses, ranging from fear and pessimism to a sense of absolute failure.

Yes, the current economic slowdown could worsen before it improves. However, recessions are neither inherently negative nor undesirable. Recessions are "contractionary" periods, encouraging us to be more prudent with our finances and expenditures, eliminate waste, and preserve resources where they are most needed. Refer to it as the yin and yang of economic cycles.

Caution: Your Beliefs About the Recession Can Be Fatal to Your Enterprise.

Our economy and businesses experience comparable boom and recession phases. Many people, including you, become sad or paralyzed by the word "recession" because of their views about recession and the meaning they assign to the phrase.

Recession IS just an issue of perspective.

Denise Corrupt.

Depending on how you perceive and respond to a recession, your business will either grow profitably or struggle for survival. Here are the top seven reasons why great organizations flourish during a recession, as well as suggestions for how you might do the same.

Even in recessionary times, the top seven reasons why great companies rise to the top are discussed.

1. The most successful businesses convert external dangers into opportunities.

The Japanese are experts in crisis management and view events such as recessions as opposites. That is, neither excellent nor terrible, but a combination of both. The Japanese character for "crisis" represents two distinct symbols: danger and opportunity. This attitude fosters receptivity rather than reactivity.

Therefore, the Japanese focus not on the problem but on innovative solutions. Not on survival but on growth. Not on short-term losses but on long-term opportunities.

How do you view the present economic slump - as a threat or an opportunity? How have you responded to earlier economic downturns?

How may the recession be an opportunity for your company?

2. Remarkable businesses take advantage of and profit from shifting market dynamics.

A corporation can develop and generate profits during a recession if it comprehends the underlying market dynamics. Crises tend to induce change in individuals. The challenge is to respond promptly and directly to such changes. To capitalize on these trends, it is essential to address the five "Ws."

WHO.

Who is currently purchasing? Purchasing habit evolves, changes, and refocuses more frequently than it decreases. Although total spending may decline, these trends cannot be generalized across all industries and business sectors. Which up-and-coming new markets can you address?

WHAT.

Which demands and perks are currently most important to your customers? Exist any new products or services that could address these transitions or act as viable alternatives to the existing quo?

WHEN.

What needs must the customer have met immediately as opposed to later? What unique incentives will encourage consumers to purchase today?

WHERE.

During a recession, customers frequently reconsider their purchasing preferences. What suppliers do they currently purchase from? How can your items be made more accessible to your target market?

WHY.

The "why" addresses the underlying buying motivations of clients. What factors currently influence the purchasing decisions of consumers? What future expectations do customers have? How will these expectations impact their current purchasing behavior?

3. Great businesses transform "bad" circumstances into good developments.

In times of economic downturn, successful businesses search for "the silver lining in the cloud" and mobilize their resources to capture these opportunities. They do not react but rather act.

Winners know that their future is not dictated by external events but by how they react to them. They focus on what they can control and respond proactively to what they cannot.

What proactive steps can you take rather than reacting to the economic downturn? How could you employ your resources more effectively to grab untapped growth and profit opportunities?

4. Great businesses generate ways for fresh growth by "decluttering" marginal or useless assets.

During periods of expansion and progress, it is easy to become addicted to overspending, "overdoing," and overconfidence. Often, sloppy behaviors, attitudes, and habits are concealed. Businesses frequently become ignorant of vital fundamentals and "waste."

Great businesses take advantage of slow periods to rid themselves of "excess" — i.e., any drains on time, money, or human resources that generate little or no return. They create space for further expansion and revenues. To be at their best, they focus on their strengths.

What expenses, projects, or activities are draining the resources of your business? Which items, services, or consumers impede the profits flow and must be eliminated? What operational "fat" must you trim to become a lean and profitable business, particularly amid the current economic downturn?

5. Great businesses hone their resilience muscles to prosper during difficult times.

Accelerating change, rising complexity, and escalating dangers have become the new corporate reality in the 21st century. A corporation must develop resilience to endure external shocks that can damage it.

Initially, resilience is a mentality. Resilience thinking transforms doubt into assurance, fear into action, and hardship into an advantage. On an organizational level, resilience results from a robust culture focused on operational flexibility, personnel loyalty, and teamwork.

Great businesses do not just recover from a single crisis or setback. They develop their resiliency. They develop the ability to anticipate the unanticipated and continually reinvent business models and tactics as conditions evolve.

How resilient is your organization in bouncing back from crises or setbacks on a scale from 1 to 10?

What efforts can you take today to enhance your capacity to anticipate and respond to the unexpected tomorrow?

6. During economic downturns, great businesses aggressively position themselves ahead of the competition.

Most businesses go on the defensive to survive economic downturns, slashing expenses, reducing marketing efforts, and commoditizing products and services.

Contrariwise, great firms do the opposite. They position themselves to succeed during a recession by increasing promotions, accelerating the release of new products, and maintaining visibility. By seizing emerging chances, businesses differentiate themselves during the recession and position themselves for exponential expansion once the economy recovers.

Currently, is your company taking an offensive or defensive stance? What three aggressive methods may your firm implement to maintain its market presence? How may your competitors' defensive responses offer you fresh growth and profit opportunities?

7. Remarkable businesses discover the "learning" and "grander purpose" concealed within difficult situations.

Our biggest obstacles are our most valuable instructors. Their "grander purpose" is to influence our thoughts, behaviors, tactics, and activities to facilitate our future development.

Companies negatively harmed by a recession can never comprehend the greater purpose that such a period might provide. Instead, they only see the negative, react out of fear, and adopt a victim mentality.

In contrast, great businesses view recessions as learning opportunities. They acknowledge that the thoughts and techniques of the past are insufficient to handle the issues of today.

Recessions encourage these organizations to get closer to their customers, reevaluate their course, and take innovative action. Their ascent to the top is frequently a result of their ideas, attitudes, and answers to such difficult circumstances.

How are your thoughts and strategies from yesterday holding you back today? What new perspectives and behaviors must you embrace to flourish in the current economic downturn? How might your organization improve as a result of the recession?

A recession might be a blessing in disguise if viewed in the proper context. At least 85 percent of your company's survival or success during a recession is within your control. You control how you see, react to, and learn and develop from it. Those companies that succeed will ascend to the top. Will you join their ranks?

CHAPTER 11: GROW YOUR BUSINESS REGARDLESS OF MARKET CONDITIONS.

People around are becoming small squirrels. They are collecting their nuts and seeds in preparation for "spring." Because they don't want to be left with nothing when the economy recovers, they forego opportunities to preserve their remaining resources. This is the incorrect action to take at this time. People should strengthen their financial status but not hide money in their beds and bury their heads in the sand.

Prepare For The Recession.

Create a clear and concise plan outlining your aims and objectives for the next three years as your first step. Include a comprehensive snapshot of your current financial situation in your plan.

You have some work to do if you have not tracked your monthly income and expenses. You can't make any changes before you know your current situation. After establishing a baseline, you can decide where you want to be in three years.

Consider the amount of money you'd like to earn and the items you'd like to have in your life, such as a new car, home, toys, charitable donations, money for your child's school, etc. Once you have considered these factors, calculate the costs associated with each of them.

With your current financial picture and your "dream" list finished, you can determine how much you need to earn over the next three years to achieve your goals. The more cash you desire, the more service or "effort" you will be forced to provide.

Implementing The Plan.

You will want to incorporate debt reduction and wealth accumulation into your plan. Allocate your existing money to these objectives in a manner that is comfortable for you. Include a monthly repeating sum when opening a business or investment account.

If you simply focus on eliminating debt, you will act on business prospects until all your debt has been paid off. This cycle is ineffective. You will never be able to work on your goals and aspirations without funds.

We are all familiar with the debt cycle. Just as you are about to finish paying off your debts, the car breaks down, or someone needs braces. You can invest and expand your business by saving monthly money in a wealth-building account.

Moving Forward While Others Are Retreating.

As your wealth-building account grows, you should look for deals and opportunities to expand your business or launch a new one. Currently, one example would be advisors for job seekers. As the employment market contracts, more and more individuals need assistance distinguishing themselves from other applicants.

There are many methods by which an entrepreneur could assist people in finding and getting employment. You must also be on the lookout for novel approaches to improve the stuff you employ often. New and improved items will always find a market. Also, start paying close attention to the market behavior of millionaires and, more essentially, billionaires.

In times of economic turmoil, many individuals amass immense riches. If you pay great attention, they will provide a wealth of information on reliable companies and areas in which it would be prudent to invest. It all depends on how you think and how well you are prepared to face obstacles head-on.

Enhancing Your Capabilities And Mindset.

Enhancing your knowledge and, more importantly, your self-confidence is one of the essential things you can do to raise your earning potential. Reading a book or seeing a motivational film each week might give you the confidence to pursue your objectives.

While you sit around whining about the economy, nothing occurs. People who are unafraid to invest in themselves and take action even while others hide from the world will be rewarded in this new era.

Finally, consider the type of life you aspire to lead and how you are already living. Do you believe that your existing habits, activities, and ideas are congruent with the life you wish to create? What can be done to bring these three elements into harmony?

Once you change your habits, actions, and beliefs, your entire life will transform, and you will be able to create the wealth you deserve.

Finally, consider the type of life you aspire to lead and how you are already living.

Do you believe that your existing habits, activities, and ideas are congruent with the life you wish to create?

What steps can you take to align these three elements?

Once you change your habits, actions, and beliefs, your entire life will transform, and you will be able to create the wealth you deserve. Set a daily goal to learn something new from these books. It will change your worldview.

CHAPTER 12: CONCENTRATE ON INNOVATION, NOT RECESSION.

The world has just evolved. The old world of financial services no longer exists, and as a result, many of the employment prospects you were pursuing may have vanished.

The promotion you were seeking may no longer be available. The bonus for which you have toiled for nine months may not materialize. Perhaps the bank you desired to work for no longer exists. The long-term departure strategy you had in mind may suddenly appear unrealistic.

Does that imply only gloom and doom? For certain individuals, perhaps. But for those who are forward-thinking, this is a fantastic opportunity to reinvent themselves instead of fretting about all the news reports of recession and decline.

As financial institutions undergo the arduous process of reinventing themselves to meet the demands of a world with more regulation, lower profits, and slower growth, you should be focused on reinventing yourself and your career, regardless of whether you have been affected by restructuring and layoffs.

Three times throughout my career, I have remade myself. Each time, a difficult market has been the catalyst. Each time, the difficult event turned out to be the best thing in my professional life.

Although it may not feel that way at the moment, the current market could be the finest thing that has ever happened to you.

Here are five strategies I've discovered for redesigning your profession in a challenging economy:

1. Stay current (within reason)

You should be aware of what is happening in the marketplace to adapt to the ever-changing demands. But you do not need to read every written dire prognostication.

Consuming excessive apocalyptic news articles and frightening prophecies will paralyze you with fear, causing you to do nothing. "Doing nothing" is a poor strategy in a world where everything changes rapidly.

2. Keep your attention on your advantages.

Every bank rationalizes its operations to concentrate on its core activity, where it is ideally positioned to give the most value to the market. This is precisely what you should be doing right now: focusing on reinventing yourself around your main assets and distinctive abilities and then providing them to organizations (your own and others) who can benefit from them.

3. Focus on fun.

You read that correctly: "fun."

Attempting to reinvent yourself into a role that you believe you should or that others believe "would be good for you" is not a good idea. Any transformation process entails arduous effort, encountering obstacles, and enduring setbacks. If you are pursuing something for which you have little passion, you have a limited chance of overcoming setbacks or conquering obstacles.

Focus instead on identifying roles that incorporate activities you enjoy. Jobs that utilize the abilities you appreciate using and allow you to work with the others you enjoy interacting with.

4. Experiment considerably more.

Some individuals know that they wish to transform themselves and their jobs but do not know how.

Here's a secret, though: you don't need to know. The only way to determine the answer is to conduct experiments. Observe someone, offer your services as a volunteer, and try out a variety of professions. Then, begin to observe what you're drawn to; what you're drawn to is usually a good indicator of the type of thing you should be transitioning into.

5. Maintain your focus on the dream.

Most people have at least one dream. A vision or big plan for their desired future lifestyle. It is something that delights and terrifies them simultaneously. This is the moment to pay attention to that dream. A challenging market is an opportunity to realize your dream; innovation is the vehicle that will carry you there far faster than you ever dreamed.

So tell me, what dream have you always kept to yourself? How can you use the process of reinvention you're about to undertake to stay on track with your compelling vision? Can you proceed with the action at this time?

Your Research.

Schedule 60 minutes in your calendar over the following few days to evaluate this list and get started on your reinvention. Before you respond, "I don't have the time," I'd want to remind you that it's not about 'time,' but priorities. Now is the perfect time to put yourself first and invest in your personal development to ensure that you are prepared for a new market.

The word 'reinvention' sounds like a term reserved for politicians, performers, and entertainment figures. However, this is not the case. We all remake ourselves throughout our lives and jobs. The process of reinvention is integral to your growth and development. Regarding your career, you are merely transitioning from one chapter to the next.

In the globalized and interconnected world in which we now reside, restructuring is a part of everyone's career. As a result, we will all have significantly more career chapters than previous generations. Consequently, you may have many more stories to share with your grandchildren when you retire.

So, even though the financial world may have shifted in the past two weeks, view the current state of the industry and economy as an opportunity to launch the next phase of your career. A chance to write your own story rather than having your employer or headline writers do it for you.

CHAPTER 13: STRATEGIES FOR INCREASING SALES DURING A RECESSION.

People and businesses have not entirely ceased spending. They are simply more discerning and risk-averse in their purchasing decisions.

If you employ these four astute techniques to combat the recession, you will escape it unscathed.

Four Recession-Defying Marketing Strategies.

1. Include a no-risk introductory offer. For instance, the online shopping cart I use offers a free 30-day trial. You can sign up, configure the shopping cart and use it for real transactions without paying until the 30th day. (At that point, you're addicted!)

The buyer may return all items before the 30th day and won't be charged. For non-monthly services, you can collect the customer's credit card information or a check in advance, guaranteeing not to charge the card or return the bill if the customer isn't satisfied.

2. Create and market informational items. Information products provide prospective clients with a low-risk, low-commitment way to get to know and eventually trust a provider. You can sell them to do-it-yourselfers who may not be able to afford full service and to frequent customers interested in learning about a new subject.

In addition to providing another revenue stream during the crisis, the information products will continue to do so when the economy recovers (as it certainly will) with no other effort. Start small, such as with brief, downloadable reports or audio recordings of expert interviews, to have things ready for sale within a matter of weeks.

3. Determine their pulse. What do your clients need most immediately?

Pay attention to the earth. Observe your target audience's complaints, queries, and desires in email discussion groups and online forums. Add a new product or service or modify a current one based on your learning about their issues.

Let's assume you notice more questions than usual on financial forums from couples nearing retirement or parents with multiple children in college. You might easily construct seminars, reports, and telephone hotline hours catered to these specific populations.

4. Pursue public relations. Invest a little effort in understanding what makes newsworthiness in the eyes of the media and use pitch letters and press releases to promote your company or yourself. To get media coverage, simply call the news desk of your metropolitan newspaper or television station and explain why you are the local aspect of today's major issue.

During a recession, you can have a higher chance of achieving 15 minutes of fame because your competitors may have reduced their PR agency retainer. Google "press release makeover service" to find a cost-effective compromise between creating your releases and asking someone else to do it for you.

Instead of listening to individuals running around wailing that the sky is falling, you could use these recession-savvy methods. You will look back on the times of doom and gloom with a smile and a huge bankroll.

CONCLUSION.

Everywhere you turn, you hear that the economy is either entering a recession, is currently on the verge of a depression, or is in a recession. It is enough to drive one insane. While it is true that financial difficulties exist in the world today, it is also true that the constant discussion of financial catastrophes contributes to the development of these conditions.

When people only hear how horrible the economy is, that layoffs are impending and that we will have money issues for months, if not years, they become reluctant to spend. When individuals don't spend money, the economy declines. It turns out to be a self-fulfilling prophecy.

How can you properly handle these difficult economic circumstances we all face? Here are some helpful suggestions.

Stay away from the media's fear and doom.

I typically watch the news on television or listen to it while driving. The frequent flood of negative information made it impossible for me to remain optimistic about my financial situation. I became increasingly apprehensive about the future. I have chosen to disconnect from the media. I refuse to read or hear about how terrible things are. Consequently, I am considerably more positive about my future.

If you are anxious about the world's current situation, you can wish to avoid publications that constantly assert that the end of the world is imminent. Don't worry - you will be informed if something truly significant occurs.

Recognize that your achievement isn't the result of chance.

The success you are currently experiencing is a result of who you are. It isn't by chance. It isn't only a matter of luck because you have labored to create value for others and are now reaping the benefits of your efforts.

The fact that economic conditions shift doesn't indicate that your success will vanish from under you. You have a success consciousness, which will aid you in achieving success in the ever-changing economic climate.

According to an old proverb, if you took all the money and divided it equally, the billionaires would quickly become millionaires again because they have a success and prosperity mindset. Your success is the outcome of your consciousness; nobody can take it away from you unless you permit them to.

Picture your ongoing success.

Maintain a mental image of yourself as a successful person. Observe others presenting you with excellent opportunities that result in abundant rewards. Does this seem unbelievable? It's not. It is a highly effective success technique. Ralph Waldo

Emerson stated, "We become what we think about throughout the day."

We all act according to how we perceive ourselves in our minds. Maintaining a mental image of your accomplishment will subconsciously signal to others that you are successful. Your continuing prosperity will inevitably ensue.

It isn't simple, but it is worthwhile.

If you believe this is simple, you are mistaken. With all the chatter about the property market decline, I may be insane. However, it's conceivable. However, my own experience and the experiences of other successful people have shown me that when we manage our minds, we control our destinies.

According to William James, "the greatest revolution of our time is the realization that people may change the outside features of their life by changing the inner attitudes of their minds." It was accurate when William James said it and remains accurate now. Recession-proof your mindset so you can continue to enjoy all that life has to offer.

Management Skills for Managers.

- Time Management for Managers
- Employee Coaching for Managers
- Team Building for Managers
- Self Confidence for Managers
- Negotiation Skills for Managers
- Customer Service Skills for Managers
- Assertiveness for Managers
- Business Etiquette for Managers
- Listening Skills for Managers
- Leadership Skills for Managers
- Communication Skills for Managers
- Presentation Skills for Managers
- Stress Management for Managers
- Decision Making for Managers
- Conflict Management for Managers.

Series: Financial Freedom at Any Age.

- Achieving Financial Freedom in your 20's
- Achieving Financial Freedom in your 30's
- Achieving Financial Freedom in your 40's
- Achieving Financial Freedom in your 50's
- Achieving Financial Freedom in your 60's
- Achieving Financial Freedom in your 70's and beyond.
- Achieving Financial Freedom in children
- Achieving Financial Freedom in teenagers
- Achieving Financial Freedom in college students.
- Financial Scams to be Aware of in Retirement.

Series: Personal Finance for You.
- Buying and Selling Crypto for Beginners
- Why Investing in Dividend Stocks Makes Sense.

Series: Wealth 2022.

- Online Entrepreneurship.
- Starting Your Own Business
- Wealth Management
- Passive Income.
- 12 Steps to Starting your own business.

Series: Excellent Customer Service.
- Excellent Customer Service in Retail
- Excellent Customer Service in Fast Food
- Excellent Customer Service in Full-Service Restaurant
- Excellent Customer Service in Teaching.
- Excellent Customer Service in Real Estate
- Excellent Customer Service in a Call Center
- Excellent Customer Service as a Receptionist
- Excellent Customer Service in a Hotel
- Excellent Customer Service in Selling
- Excellent Customer Service No Matter the Situation.

- Excellent Customer Service in Dental Office
- Excellent Customer Service in Medical Office.

Series: Quick Money.

- Quick Money in a Week
- Quick Money in a Weekend
- Quick Money in a Month
- Quick Money for Students.

Series: How to Promote.

- How to Promote your Recipe Book
- How to Promote your Children's Book.

Other books by D.K. Hawkins.

- How to Make Your Business Thrive During a Recession
- Creating Surplus Value for Customers
- Recognizing Opportunities to Increase Cash Flow.
- Recessions are When Millionaires and Billionaires are Created.

Author Bio

D.K. Hawkins. D.K. enjoys reading personal business books as well as spending time outdoors. More books will come in this collection, so please follow on Amazon for more books.

Thank you for your purchase of this book.

I honestly do appreciate it and appreciate you, my excellent customer.

God Bless You.

D.K. Hawkins.